Saying goodbye to...

A Brother or Sister

Chrysalis Children's Books

First published in the UK in 2003 by
Chrysalis Children's Books
An imprint of Chrysalis Books Group Plc
The Chrysalis Building
Bramley Road
London W10 6SP

Paperback edition first published in 2005

Text by Nicola Edwards

Editorial manager: Joyce Bentley
Senior editor: Sarah Nunn
Project editor: Jean Coppendale
Designer: Clare Sleven
Illustrations by: Sarah Roper
Picture researcher: Jenny Barlow
Consultant: Jenni Thomas, Chief Executive The
Child Bereavement Trust

ISBN 1 84138 835 1 (hb)
ISBN 1 84458 465 8 (pb)

British Library Cataloguing in Publication
Data for this book is available from the British
Library.

Printed in China

Foreword

Confronting death and dying as an adult is difficult but addressing these issues with children is even harder. Children need to hear the truth and sharing a book can encourage and help both adults and children to talk openly and honestly about their feelings, something many of us find difficult to do.

Written in a clear, sensitive and very caring way, the **Saying Goodbye To...** series will help parents, carers and teachers to meet the needs of grieving children. Reading about the variety of real life situations, including the death of a pet, may enable children to feel less alone and more able to make sense of the bewildering emotions and responses they feel when someone dies.

Being alongside grieving children is not easy, the **Saying Goodbye To...** series will help make this challenging task a little less daunting.

Jenni Thomas OBE
Chief Executive
The Child Bereavement Trust

The Child Bereavement Trust
Registered Charity No. 04049

All reasonable efforts have been made to trace the relevant copyright holders of the images contained within this book. If we were unable to reach you, please contact Chrysalis Children's Books.

Cover Getty Images/Photodisc/SW Productions 1 Bubbles/Frans-Rombout 4 Bubbles/Peter Sylent 5 Bubbles/Jennie Woodcock 6 Corbis/Mug Shots 7 Bubbles/Jennie Woodcock 8 Bubbles/Denise Hager 9 Bubbles/Loisjoy Thurston 10 Photofusion/Brian Mitchell 11 Bubbles/Angela Hampton 12 Corbis/John Henley 13 Bubbles/Loisjoy Thurston 14 Bubbles/Ian West 15 Getty Images/Photodisc/Adam Crowley 16 Bubbles/Angela Hampton 17 Bubbles/Frans-Rombout 18 Getty Images/Eyewire Collection 19 Getty Images/John Lamb 20 Corbis/Ted Horowitz 21 Bubbles/Jennie Woodcock 22 Bubbles/Chris Rout 23 Getty Images/Photodisc/SW Productions 24 Getty Images/Photodisc/Buccina Studios 25 Corbis/Ed Quinn 26 Getty Images/Photodisc/SW Productions 27 Getty Images/Grant V. Faint 28 Bubbles/Jennie Woodcock 29 Bubbles/Chris Rout.

Contents

Hard to bear

Children usually think of death as something that happens to an old person at the end of a long life. When a baby or a child dies people feel very shocked. It's very hard to understand and to bear. The sadness that a child's death brings to a family affects lots of people for a long time.

When a child dies it seems so wrong and unfair. It is usually older people who die, not children.

When Jon died, Jamie kept some of Jon's things to remind him of his brother.

Something to think about...
If you are feeling sad because your brother or sister has died, it can help to talk about how you're feeling with someone you **trust** and who understands.

5

Illness

Some children are seriously ill for a time before they die. They may have to spend a lot of time in hospital or in a **hospice** where their families and friends can visit them. Knowing that someone is going to die still makes their death very hard to understand. It's difficult to believe that they're not going to be around any more.

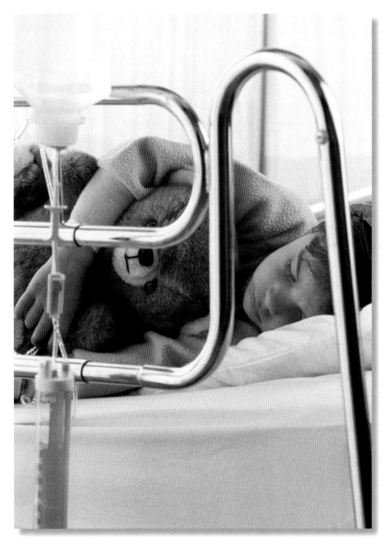

When Clare was in hospital, her brother Dominic came to visit her. Clare liked to hear how her favourite football team was getting on.

Erin was very sad when her brother, Oscar, died. Her mum cuddled Erin and **comforted** her.

Something to think about...
If a child you know has died, it's normal to worry that you might fall ill and die, too. But most people get better if they've been ill and live a long life.

7

A terrible shock

Sometimes a child dies suddenly and unexpectedly. When this happens, people are suddenly plunged into shock. No one has any time to prepare for how they are going to feel. It may be difficult to believe that the child has died. The shock can make people feel frightened, or helpless or just **numb**.

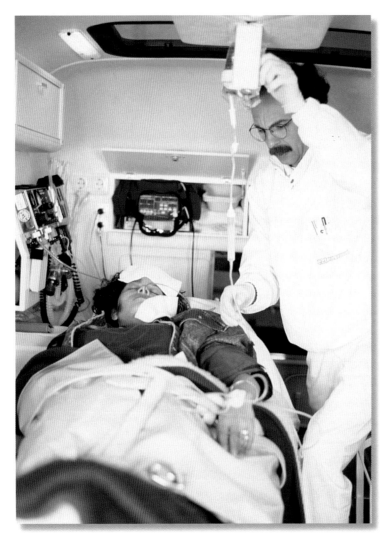

Every year, throughout the world, some children are killed crossing the road or as passengers in car accidents.

Something to think about...
When a child dies suddenly, there are people around who are trained to offer the family help and support the family in their **bereavement**.

A new baby can bring a lot of happiness to a family. But when a baby dies, everyone in the family has to cope with knowing that they will not see them grow up.

Why them?

Children who are mourning the death of a brother or sister have a mixture of feelings. They may feel confused or angry that the death has happened. They may also feel very upset with their parents for not being able to stop it happening.

When Zina's brother died she lost her temper with her best friend. She thought that Anna couldn't understand how she was feeling.

They may even feel angry with their brother or sister for dying and leaving them to feel so sad and **lonely**.

David didn't know anyone else whose brother or sister had died because not many children die. It made him feel lost and lonely.

Feeling guilty

Children often feel **guilty** when their brother or sister dies. They may worry that they might have done something to cause the death. They may wish they'd said or done something differently while their brother or sister was still alive.

Jessica felt guilty when her brother Alex died. She'd been **jealous** of the attention that everyone paid him when he was ill.

They may also feel bad because they had **quarrelled** with them, or if they hadn't had a proper chance to say goodbye.

After Zak died his sister, Molly, wished she'd been nicer to him. She remembered the times when they used to argue and felt sad that she hadn't played with Zak very much.

Something to think about...
When a child dies it's natural for their brother or sister to feel guilty. They may even think that it's their fault in some way. They may worry that it's unfair because they are still alive. Children need to be **reassured** that it's not their fault if their brother or sister has died.

Sad and lonely

Some children feel better if they can cry when they're feeling very sad. Crying can be a way of letting out feelings of sadness. But not all children can cry, even when they want to. Some children don't feel like crying at all. Everyone **grieves** in their own way.

It helped Anita to draw a picture of her sister.

16

Saying goodbye to a brother or sister

Leanne felt so lonely when her brother, Jason, died. She couldn't believe she'd never see him again.

17

Asking questions

Sometimes when someone dies, adults may try to **protect** children by not explaining exactly what has happened. They may even try to avoid talking about it at all. But this can make children even more confused and upset. It's natural to want to ask lots of questions when someone dies. It's a way to try to make sense of what has happened.

When Michael's twin brother, Joe, died, everyone in their class had the chance to talk about how they would remember their friend.

When Rob's sister, Sally, died, his dad told him how much he loved and missed her.

Something to think about...
It helps children when adults are able to discuss their questions with them, even if they do not have all the answers. Then they can share their feelings with each other.

Helping each other

When a child dies lots of people in the family feel shocked and sad. Sometimes the parents may be so upset themselves that they seem to have less time for their other children.

Michael's dog helped to comfort him when his sister, Gillian, died suddenly.

Grandparents, aunts, uncles and cousins are also **grieving** but they can help children at this sad and difficult time. It can be a comfort for the family to share their feelings of sadness and loss.

It helped Lee to go back to school after his brother, Paul, died. He felt safe, because school hadn't changed and he was comfortable there.

21

Preparing for a funeral

A **funeral** is a special service which gives people who cared about the person who has died a chance to remember them and say goodbye. Some funerals are **religious**, others are not. Different people have different beliefs. It's important for children to know what they can expect to happen at a funeral. Then they can decide whether or not they would like to be part of it.

Hannah wrote a letter to her brother, Ben, to say goodbye to him. Her mum and dad put it in Ben's **coffin**.

At a funeral, people share their memories of the person who has died. By going to the funeral they show their **respect** for them.

Something to think about...

There are several ways in which you can get involved in preparing for a funeral if you would like to – for example, by helping to choose the flowers or songs or making up a prayer for the service.

Saying goodbye

At a funeral it can be strange for children to see the people that they care about looking so upset and crying. But it's natural to feel sad at a funeral. People are there to comfort each other.

When Becky died, all her friends from her class went to her funeral.

Some children choose to take part in the funeral in some way, for example by lighting a candle in memory of the person who has died. Others choose not to go and prefer to remember in their own way instead.

Chloe held a candle at her sister's funeral.

Sharing memories

It's important for children to have their own private memories of their brother or sister. But it's also important for family and friends to help each other by sharing their memories – of the things he or she used to say and do, their favourite television programmes and music, the food they liked and the places they visited.

When Stephen and Yasmin looked through photo albums with their mum and dad, it reminded them of the happy times they'd spent with their brother, James.

Something to do...
You could write down or draw pictures of the things that remind you of your brother or sister or some of the things you did together that were fun, such as going to the park or riding your bikes.

Josh and his family liked to remember his baby sister, Sarah, by going to church and lighting a candle for her on her birthday each year.

Feeling happy again

When a brother or sister dies, children notice that, although life carries on as normal, things will never be quite the same again. There will be moments when they'll suddenly feel very unhappy. Grieving is natural and it's normal for different feelings to come and go. After a while children may realise that the happy memories of their brother or sister are there more often than the sad ones. Even when someone dies they are still part of the family and they will always be remembered and loved.

When Jack played football he sometimes thought about how much his brother, Matt, used to enjoy it.

Saying goodbye to a brother or sister

Bella chose a special frame for a photo of her sister, Lydia, sitting with the rest of the family.

Something to think about...
Try not to feel guilty about enjoying yourself again – it's natural to want to have a happy time. Your brother or sister will always be important to you.

Glossary

beliefs	the different ideas that are important to each person
bereavement	what happens to a person when someone they care about dies
coffin	the container in which a dead body is placed
comfort	to help someone who is sad to feel better
funeral	a special service in which people remember a person who has died and say goodbye to them
grieving	the natural feelings of sadness after someone has died
guilty	feeling bad, as if it's your fault that something is wrong
hospice	a building where people who are dying are looked after
jealous	wishing that what someone else has could be yours
lonely	feeling sad and alone
mourning	the ways in which people who have been bereaved show their feelings of grief
numb	unable to feel anything
protect	taking care of someone, keeping them from harm
quarrel	to have an argument
reassure	to give comfort and help someone who is feeling worried
religious	to do with a belief in God
respect	thinking kindly and politely of someone
trust	to feel that someone will not let you down

Useful addresses

The Child Bereavement Trust
A charity offering training, resources and support for professional carers and teachers working with bereaved children and grieving adults
Aston House
High Street
West Wycombe
Bucks HP14 3AG
Tel: 01494 446648
Information and Support Line: 0845 357 1000
E-mail: enquiries@childbereavement.org.uk
Website: www.childbereavement.org.uk
* New interactive website where children and adults can send emails

Childhood Bereavement Network
An organization offering bereaved children and their families and caregivers information about the support services available to them.
Huntingdon House
278-290 Huntingdon Street
Nottingham NG1 3LY
Tel: 0115 911 8070
E-mail: cbn@ncb.org.uk
Website: www.ncb.org.uk/cbn

ChildLine
Childline's free, 24-hour helpline is staffed by trained counsellors, offering help and support to children and young people. The website includes information on bereavement.
Freepost 1111
London N1 0BR
Tel: 0800 11 11 (Freephone 24 hours)
Website: www.childline.org.uk

Cruse Bereavement Care
The Cruse helpline offers information and counselling to people of all ages who have been bereaved. The website offers additional information and support.

Cruse House
126 Sheen Road
Richmond
Surrey TW9 1UR
Tel: 020 8322 7227
Helpline: 0870 167 1677 (Mondays to Fridays 9.30am–5pm)
Website: www.crusebereavementcare.org.uk

The Samaritans
An organization offering support and help to anyone who is emotionally distressed.
Tel: 08457 90 90 90 (24 hours)
Website: www.samaritans.org.uk

Support in Bereavement for Brothers and Sisters (SIBBS)
An organization that can be reached via the Compassionate Friends website, offering support and help to brothers and sisters who have been bereaved.
Website: www.tcf.org.uk

Winston's Wish
A charity offering support and information to bereaved children and their families.
The Clara Burgess Centre
Gloucestershire Royal Hospital
Great Western Road
Gloucester GL1 3NN
Tel: 01452 394377
Family Line: 0845 20 30 40 5 (Mondays to Fridays 9.30am–5pm)
E-mail: info@winstonswish.org.uk
Website: www.winstonswish.org

Youth Access
An organization providing information about youth counselling services.
1-2 Taylors Yard
67 Alderbrook Road
London SW12 8AD
Tel: 020 8772 9900 (Monday to Fridays 9am–1pm, 2-5pm)
E-mail: admin@youthaccess.org.uk

Index